INAUGURAL PRESIDENTIAL ADDRESS

BY
Barack Hussein Obama

My fellow Americans, I stand before you today, humbled by the task before us, grateful for the trust bestowed, mindful of the sacrifices born by our ancestors.

I thank President Bush for his service to our nation [applause pause], as well as the generosity and cooperation he has shown throughout this transition.

44 Americans have now taken the presidential oath. Words have been spoken during rising tides of prosperity, and the still waters of peace. Yet every so often the oath is taken amidst gathering clouds, and raging storms.

At these moments, America has carried on, not simply because of the vision or skill of those in high office, but because we, the people, have remained faithful to the ideals of our forebears, and true to our founding documents. So it has been, so it must be with THIS generation of Americans.

That we are in the midst of crisis is now well understood.

Our nation is at war with a far reaching network of violence and hatred.

Our economy is badly weakened, a consequence of greed and irresponsibility on the part of some, but also our collective failure to make hard choices, and prepare the nation for a new age. Homes have been lost, jobs shed, businesses shuttered/shattered???, our health care is too costly, our schools fail too many, and each day brings brings new evidence that the way we use energy strengthens our adversaries and threatens our planet.

These are the indicators of crisis, subject to data and statistics. Less measurable, but no less profound is the sapping of confidence across our land, a nagging fear that America's decline is inevitable, that the next generation must lower its sights.

Today I say to you that the challenges we face are real. They are serious and they are many. They will not be met easily or in a short span of time, but know this America, THEY WILL BE MET! [applause pause]

On this day, we gather because we have chosen hope

over fear, unity of purpose over conflict and discord. On this day, we come to proclaim an end to the petty grievances and false promises, the recriminations, and worn out dogmas that for far too long have strangles our politics.

We remain a young nation, but in the words of scripture, the time has come to set aside childish things.

The time has come to reaffirm our enduring spirit, to choose our better history, to carry forward that precious gift, that noble idea, passed on from generation to generation, the God given promise that ALL are equal, ALL are free, and ALL deserve a chance to pursue their full measure of happiness.

[longer pause for applause]

In reaffirming the greatness of our nation, we understand that greatness is never a given.

It must be earned.

Our journey has never been one of shortcuts or settling for less.

It has not been the path for the faint hearted, for

those who prefer leisure over work, or seek only the pleasures of riches and fame, rather it has been the risk takers, the doers, the makers of things, some celebrated, but more often men and women obscure in their labor, who have carried us up the long rugged path towards prosperity and freedom.

For us, they packed up their few worldly possessions and travelled across oceans in search of a new life.

For us, they toiled in sweatshops, and settled the West, endured the lash of the whip, and plowed the hard earth.

For us, they fought, and died, in places like Concord, and Gettysburg, Normandy, and Khe Sahn.

Time and again, these men and women struggled and sacrificed until their hands were raw, so that we might live a better life.

They saw America as bigger than the sum of our individual ambitions, greater than all the differences of birth, or wealth, or faction.

THIS is the journey we continue today.

We remain the most prosperous powerful nation on Earth.

Our workers are no less productive than when this crisis began.

Our minds are no less inventive.

Our goods and services no less needed than they were last week, or last month, or last year.

Our capacity remains undiminished, but our time of standing pat, of protecting narrow interests and putting off unpleasant decisions...that time has surely passed.

Starting TODAY, we must pick ourselves up, dust ourselves off, and begin again the work of remaking America...

[long applause pause]

...for everywhere we look there is work to be done.

The state of our economy calls for action, bold and swift, and we will act, not only to create new jobs, but to lay new foundations for growth. We will build the roads and bridges, the electric grids and digital lines that feed our commerce and bind us together.

We will restore science to its rightful place, and wield

technology's wonders to raise health care's quality and lower its cost.

We will harness the sun and the winds and the soil to fuel our cars and run our factories, and we will transform our schools and colleges and universities to meet the demands of a new age.

All this we can do.

All this we WILL do.

Now, there are some who question the scale of our ambitions, who suggest that our system cannot tolerate too many big plans.

Their memories are short, for they have forgotten what this country has already done, what free men and women can achieve when imagination is joined to common purpose, and necessity to courage.

What the cynics fail to understand, is that the ground has shifted beneath them, that the stale political arguments that have consumed us for so long no longer apply.

The question we ask to day is not whether our government is too big or too small, but whether it works, whether it helps families find jobs at a decent wage, care they can afford, a retirement that is dignified. Where the answer is YES, we intend to move forward, where the answer is NO, programs will end, and those of us who manage the public's dollars will be held to account, to spend wisely, reform bad habits, and do our business in the light of day, because only then can we restore the vital trust between a people and their government.

Nor is the question before us whether the market is a force for good or ill.

Its power to generate wealth and expand freedom is unmatched, but this crisis has reminded us that without a watchful eye, the market can spin out of control, the nation cannot prosper long when it favors only the prosperous.

The success of our economy has always depended, not just on the size of our gross domestic product, but on the reach of our prosperity, on our ability to extend opportunity to every willing heart, not out of charity, but because it is the surest route to our common good.

[long applause pause]

As for our common defense, we reject as false the choice between our safety and our ideals.

Our founding fathers [pause for applause]. . . .

Our founding fathers, faced with perils we can scarcely imagine, drafted a charter to assure the rule of law and the rights of man, a charter expanded by the blood of generations. Those ideals still light the world, and we will not give them up for expedients' sake. . .

[applause pause]

. . .and so, to all the other peoples and governments who are watching today, from the grandest capitols, to the small village where my father was born, know that America is a friend of each nation, and every man, woman, and child, who seeks a future of peace and dignity, and we are ready to lead once more.

[long pause for applause]

Recall that earlier generations faced down fascism and communism, not just with missiles and tanks, but with the sturdy alliances and enduring convictions.

They understood that our power alone cannot protect us, nor does it entitle us to do as we please. Instead, they knew that our power grows through its prudent use, our security emanates from the justness of our cause, the force of our example, the tempering qualities of humility and restraint.

We are the keepers of this legacy.

Guided by these principles once more, we can meet those new threats that demand even greater effort, even greater cooperation and understanding between nations.

We will begin to responsibly leave Iraq to is people, and forge a hard earned peace in Afghanistan.

With old friends and former foes we will work tirelessly to lessen the nuclear threat, and roll back the specter of a warming planet.

We will not apologize for our way of life, nor will we waver in its defense, and for those who seek to advance their aims by inducing terror and slaughtering innocents, we say to you now, that our spirit is stronger, and cannot be broken.

You cannot outlast us, and we will defeat you!

[long pause for applause]

For we know that our patchwork heritage is a strength, not a weakness.

We are a nation of Christians and Muslims, Jews and Hindus, and non-believers. We are shaped by every language and culture, drawn from every end of this Earth, and because we have tasted the bitter swill of civil war and segregation, and emerged from that dark chapter stronger, and more united, we cannot help but believe that the old hatreds shall someday pass, that the lines of tribe shall soon dissolve, that as the world grows smaller, our common humanity shall reveal itself, and that America must play its role in ushering in a new era of peace.

To the Muslim world, we seek a new way forward, based on mutual interest and mutual respect.

To those leaders around the globe who seek to sow conflict, or blame their societies' ills on the West, know that your people will judge you on what you can build, not what you destroy.

[pause for applause]

To those who cling to power through corruption and deceit, and the silencing of dissent, know that you are on the wrong side of history, but that we will extend a hand if you are willing to unclench your fist.

[pause for applause]

To the people of poor nations, we pledge to work alongside you to make your farms flourish and let clean waters flow, to nourish starved bodies, and feed hungry minds, and to those nations like ours that enjoy relative plenty, we say we can no longer afford indifference to the suffering outside our borders, nor can we consume the world's resources without regard to effect.

For the world has changed, and we much change with it.

As we consider the road that unfolds before us, we remember with humble gratitude those brave Americans who, at this very hour, patrol far off deserts and distant mountains. They have something to tell us, just as the fallen heroes who lie in Arlington whisper through the ages. We honor them, not only because they are the guardians of our liberty, but because they embody the spirit of service, a willingness to find meaning in something greater than themselves.

And yet, at this moment, a moment that will define a generation, it is precisely this spirit that must inhabit us ALL.

For as a government can do, and must do, it us ultimately the faith and determination of the American people upon which this nation relies. It is the kindness to take in a stranger when the levees break, the selflessness of workers who would rather cut their hours than see a friend lose their job, which sees us through our darkest hours. It is the firefighters' courage to storm a stairway filled with smoke, but also a parent's willingness to nurture a child, that finally decides our fate.

Our challenges may be new, the instruments with which we meet them may be new, but those values upon which our success depends, honesty, and hard work, courage and fair play, tolerance and curiosity, loyalty and patriotism, these things are old, these things are true. They have been the quiet force of progress throughout our history.

What is demanded then, is a return to these truths.

What is required of us now, is a new era of responsibility, a recognition on the part of every American, that we have duties to ourselves, our nation, and the world, duties that we do not grudgingly accept, but rather seize gladly, firm in the knowledge that there is nothing so satisfying to the spirit, so defining of our character, than giving our all to a difficult task.

This is the price and the promise of citizenship.

This is the source of our confidence, the knowledge that God calls on us to shape an uncertain destiny.

This is the meaning of our liberty and our creed, why men and women and children of every race and every faith can join in celebration across this magnificent mall, and why a man whose father, less than 60 years ago, might not have been served at a local restaurant can now stand before you to take a most sacred oath.

[long pause for applause]

So let us mark this day with remembrance, of who we are, and how far we have traveled. In the year of America's birth, in the coldest of months, a small band of patriots huddled by dying campfires on the shores of an icy river.

The capitol was abandoned, the enemy was advancing, the snow was stained with blood. At a moment when the outcome of our revolution was most in doubt, the father of our nation ordered these words be read to the people:

"Let it be told to the future world, that in the depth of winter, when nothing but hope and virtue could survive, that the city and the country, alarmed at one common danger, came forth to meet it."

America, in the face of our common dangers, in this winter of our hardship, let us remember these timeless words. With hope and virtue, let us brave once more the icy currents, and endure what storms may come. Let it be said by our children's children, that when we were tested, we refused to let this journey end, that we did not turn back, nor did we falter, and with eyes fixed on the horizon and God's grace upon us, we carried forth that great gift of freedom and delivered it safely to future generations.

Thank you, God bless you, and God bless the United States of America.

www.bookjungle.com *email: sales@bookjungle.com fax: 630-214-0564 mail: Book Jungle PO Box 2226 Champaign, IL 61825*

The Codes Of Hammurabi And Moses
W. W. Davies

The discovery of the Hammurabi Code is one of the greatest achievements of archaeology, and is of paramount interest, not only to the student of the Bible, but also to all those interested in ancient history...

Religion   **ISBN:** *1-59462-338-4*   **Pages:** 132   *MSRP $12.95*   QTY

The Theory of Moral Sentiments
Adam Smith

This work from 1749. contains original theories of conscience amd moral judgment and it is the foundation for systemof morals.

Philosophy   **ISBN:** *1-59462-777-0*   **Pages:** 536   *MSRP $19.95*   QTY

Jessica's First Prayer
Hesba Stretton

In a screened and secluded corner of one of the many railway-bridges which span the streets of London there could be seen a few years ago, from five o'clock every morning until half past eight, a tidily set-out coffee-stall, consisting of a trestle and board, upon which stood two large tin cans, with a small fire of charcoal burning under each so as to keep the coffee boiling during the early hours of the morning when the work-people were thronging into the city on their way to their daily toil...

Childrens   **ISBN:** *1-59462-373-2*   **Pages:** 84   *MSRP $9.95*   QTY

My Life and Work
Henry Ford

Henry Ford revolutionized the world with his implementation of mass production for the Model T automobile. Gain valuable business insight into his life and work with his own auto-biography... "We have only started on our development of our country we have not as yet, with all our talk of wonderful progress, done more than scratch the surface. The progress has been wonderful enough but..."

Biographies/   **ISBN:** *1-59462-198-5*   **Pages:** 300   *MSRP $21.95*   QTY

www.bookjungle.com email: sales@bookjungle.com fax: 630-214-0564 mail: Book Jungle PO Box 2226 Champaign, IL 61825

The Art of Cross-Examination
Francis Wellman

QTY

I presume it is the experience of every author, after his first book is published upon an important subject, to be almost overwhelmed with a wealth of ideas and illustrations which could readily have been included in his book, and which to his own mind, at least, seem to make a second edition inevitable. Such certainly was the case with me; and when the first edition had reached its sixth impression in five months, I rejoiced to learn that it seemed to my publishers that the book had met with a sufficiently favorable reception to justify a second and considerably enlarged edition. ..

Reference   ISBN: *1-59462-647-2*   Pages:412   MSRP *$19.95*

On the Duty of Civil Disobedience
Henry David Thoreau

QTY

Thoreau wrote his famous essay, On the Duty of Civil Disobedience, as a protest against an unjust but popular war and the immoral but popular institution of slave-owning. He did more than write—he declined to pay his taxes, and was hauled off to gaol in consequence. Who can say how much this refusal of his hastened the end of the war and of slavery?

Law   ISBN: *1-59462-747-9*   Pages:48   MSRP *$7.45*

Dream Psychology Psychoanalysis for Beginners
Sigmund Freud

QTY

Sigmund Freud, born Sigismund Schlomo Freud (May 6, 1856 - September 23, 1939), was a Jewish-Austrian neurologist and psychiatrist who co-founded the psychoanalytic school of psychology. Freud is best known for his theories of the unconscious mind, especially involving the mechanism of repression; his redefinition of sexual desire as mobile and directed towards a wide variety of objects; and his therapeutic techniques, especially his understanding of transference in the therapeutic relationship and the presumed value of dreams as sources of insight into unconscious desires.

Psychology   ISBN: *1-59462-905-6*   Pages:196   MSRP *$15.45*

The Miracle of Right Thought
Orison Swett Marden

QTY

Believe with all of your heart that you will do what you were made to do. When the mind has once formed the habit of holding cheerful, happy, prosperous pictures, it will not be easy to form the opposite habit. It does not matter how improbable or how far away this realization may see, or how dark the prospects may be, if we visualize them as best we can, as vividly as possible, hold tenaciously to them and vigorously struggle to attain them, they will gradually become actualized, realized in the life. But a desire, a longing without endeavor, a yearning abandoned or held indifferently will vanish without realization.

Self Help   ISBN: *1-59462-644-8*   Pages:360   MSRP *$25.45* www.bookjungle.com *email: sales@bookjungle.com fax: 630-214-0564 mail: Book Jungle PO Box 2226 Champaign, IL 61825*

QTY

- [ ] **The Rosicrucian Cosmo-Conception Mystic Christianity** *by Max Heindel* ISBN: *1-59462-188-8* **$38.95**
  The Rosicrucian Cosmo-conception is not dogmatic, neither does it appeal to any other authority than the reason of the student. It is; not controversial, but is: sent forth in the, hope that it may help to clear... New Age/Religion Pages 646

- [ ] **Abandonment To Divine Providence** *by Jean-Pierre de Caussade* ISBN: *1-59462-228-0* **$25.95**
  "The Rev. Jean Pierre de Caussade was one of the most remarkable spiritual writers of the Society of Jesus in France in the 18th Century. His death took place at Toulouse in 1751. His works have gone through many editions and have been republished... Inspirational/Religion Pages 400

- [ ] **Mental Chemistry** *by Charles Haanel* ISBN: *1-59462-192-6* **$23.95**
  Mental Chemistry allows the change of material conditions by combining and appropriately utilizing the power of the mind. Much like applied chemistry creates something new and unique out of careful combinations of chemicals the mastery of mental chemistry... New Age Pages 354

- [ ] **The Letters of Robert Browning and Elizabeth Barret Barrett 1845-1846 vol II** ISBN: *1-59462-193-4* **$35.95**
  by Robert Browning and Elizabeth Barrett Biographies Pages 596

- [ ] **Gleanings In Genesis (volume I)** *by Arthur W. Pink* ISBN: *1-59462-130-6* **$27.45**
  Appropriately has Genesis been termed "the seed plot of the Bible" for in it we have, in germ form, almost all of the great doctrines which are afterwards fully developed in the books of Scripture which follow... Religion/Inspirational Pages 420

- [ ] **The Master Key** *by L. W. de Laurence* ISBN: *1-59462-001-6* **$30.95**
  In no branch of human knowledge has there been a more lively increase of the spirit of research during the past few years than in the study of Psychology, Concentration and Mental Discipline. The requests for authentic lessons in Thought Control, Mental Discipline and... New Age/Business Pages 422

- [ ] **The Lesser Key Of Solomon Goetia** *by L. W. de Laurence* ISBN: *1-59462-092-X* **$9.95**
  This translation of the first book of the "Lernegton" which is now for the first time made accessible to students of Talismanic Magic was done, after careful collation and edition, from numerous Ancient Manuscripts in Hebrew, Latin, and French... New Age/Occult Pages 92

- [ ] **Rubaiyat Of Omar Khayyam** *by Edward Fitzgerald* ISBN: *1-59462-332-5* **$13.95**
  Edward Fitzgerald, whom the world has already learned, in spite of his own efforts to remain within the shadow of anonymity, to look upon as one of the rarest poets of the century, was born at Bredfield, in Suffolk, on the 31st of March, 1809. He was the third son of John Purcell... Music Pages 172

- [ ] **Ancient Law** *by Henry Maine* ISBN: *1-59462-128-4* **$29.95**
  The chief object of the following pages is to indicate some of the earliest ideas of mankind, as they are reflected in Ancient Law, and to point out the relation of those ideas to modern thought. Religiom/History Pages 452

- [ ] **Far-Away Stories** *by William J. Locke* ISBN: *1-59462-129-2* **$19.45**
  "Good wine needs no bush, but a collection of mixed vintages does. And this book is just such a collection. Some of the stories I do not want to remain buried for ever in the museum files of dead magazine-numbers an author's not unpardonable vanity..." Fiction Pages 272

- [ ] **Life of David Crockett** *by David Crockett* ISBN: *1-59462-250-7* **$27.45**
  "Colonel David Crockett was one of the most remarkable men of the times in which he lived. Born in humble life, but gifted with a strong will, an indomitable courage, and unremitting perseverance... Biographies/New Age Pages 424

- [ ] **Lip-Reading** *by Edward Nitchie* ISBN: *1-59462-206-X* **$25.95**
  Edward B. Nitchie, founder of the New York School for the Hard of Hearing, now the Nitchie School of Lip-Reading, Inc, wrote "LIP-READING Principles and Practice". The development and perfecting of this meritorious work on lip-reading was an undertaking... How-to Pages 400

- [ ] **A Handbook of Suggestive Therapeutics, Applied Hypnotism, Psychic Science** ISBN: *1-59462-214-0* **$24.95**
  by Henry Munro Health/New Age/Health/Self-help Pages 376

- [ ] **A Doll's House: and Two Other Plays** *by Henrik Ibsen* ISBN: *1-59462-112-8* **$19.95**
  Henrik Ibsen created this classic when in revolutionary 1848 Rome. Introducing some striking concepts in playwriting for the realist genre, this play has been studied the world over. Fiction/Classics/Plays 308

- [ ] **The Light of Asia** *by sir Edwin Arnold* ISBN: *1-59462-204-3* **$13.95**
  In this poetic masterpiece, Edwin Arnold describes the life and teachings of Buddha. The man who was to become known as Buddha to the world was born as Prince Gautama of India but he rejected the worldly riches and abandoned the reigns of power when... Religion/History/Biographies Pages 170

- [ ] **The Complete Works of Guy de Maupassant** *by Guy de Maupassant* ISBN: *1-59462-157-8* **$16.95**
  "For days and days, nights and nights, I had dreamed of that first kiss which was to consecrate our engagement, and I knew not on what spot I should put my lips..." Fiction/Classics Pages 240

- [ ] **The Art of Cross-Examination** *by Francis L. Wellman* ISBN: *1-59462-309-0* **$26.95**
  Written by a renowned trial lawyer, Wellman imparts his experience and uses case studies to explain how to use psychology to extract desired information through questioning. How-to/Science/Reference Pages 408

- [ ] **Answered or Unanswered?** *by Louisa Vaughan* ISBN: *1-59462-248-5* **$10.95**
  Miracles of Faith in China Religion Pages 112

- [ ] **The Edinburgh Lectures on Mental Science (1909)** *by Thomas* ISBN: *1-59462-008-3* **$11.95**
  This book contains the substance of a course of lectures recently given by the writer in the Queen Street Hall, Edinburgh. Its purpose is to indicate the Natural Principles governing the relation between Mental Action and Material Conditions... New Age/Psychology Pages 148

- [ ] **Ayesha** *by H. Rider Haggard* ISBN: *1-59462-301-5* **$24.95**
  Verily and indeed it is the unexpected that happens! Probably if there was one person upon the earth from whom the Editor of this, and of a certain previous history, did not expect to hear again... Classics Pages 380

- [ ] **Ayala's Angel** *by Anthony Trollope* ISBN: *1-59462-352-X* **$29.95**
  The two girls were both pretty, but Lucy who was twenty-one who supposed to be simple and comparatively unattractive, whereas Ayala was credited, as her Bombwhat romantic name might show, with poetic charm and a taste for romance. Ayala when her father died was nineteen... Fiction Pages 484

- [ ] **The American Commonwealth** *by James Bryce* ISBN: *1-59462-286-8* **$34.45**
  An interpretation of American democratic political theory. It examines political mechanics and society from the perspective of Scotsman James Bryce Politics Pages 572

- [ ] **Stories of the Pilgrims** *by Margaret P. Pumphrey* ISBN: *1-59462-116-0* **$17.95**
  This book explores pilgrims religious oppression in England as well as their escape to Holland and eventual crossing to America on the Mayflower, and their early days in New England... History Pages 268

www.bookjungle.com *email:* sales@bookjungle.com *fax:* 630-214-0564 *mail:* Book Jungle PO Box 2226 Champaign, IL 61825

QTY

The Fasting Cure *by Sinclair Upton* ISBN: *1-59462-222-1* **$13.95**
In the Cosmopolitan Magazine for May, 1910, and in the Contemporary Review (London) for April, 1910, I published an article dealing with my experiences in fasting. I have written a great many magazine articles, but never one which attracted so much attention... *New Age/Self Help/Health Pages 164*

Hebrew Astrology *by Sepharial* ISBN: *1-59462-308-2* **$13.45**
In these days of advanced thinking it is a matter of common observation that we have left many of the old landmarks behind and that we are now pressing forward to greater heights and to a wider horizon than that which represented the mind-content of our progenitors... *Astrology Pages 144*

Thought Vibration or The Law of Attraction in the Thought World ISBN: *1-59462-127-6* **$12.95**
by William Walker Atkinson *Psychology/Religion Pages 144*

Optimism *by Helen Keller* ISBN: *1-59462-108-X* **$15.95**
Helen Keller was blind, deaf, and mute since 19 months old, yet famously learned how to overcome these handicaps, communicate with the world, and spread her lectures promoting optimism. An inspiring read for everyone... *Biographies/Inspirational Pages 84*

Sara Crewe *by Frances Burnett* ISBN: *1-59462-360-0* **$9.45**
In the first place, Miss Minchin lived in London. Her home was a large, dull, tall one, in a large, dull square, where all the houses were alike, and all the sparrows were alike, and where all the door-knockers made the same heavy sound... *Childrens/Classic Pages 88*

The Autobiography of Benjamin Franklin *by Benjamin Franklin* ISBN: *1-59462-135-7* **$24.95**
The Autobiography of Benjamin Franklin has probably been more extensively read than any other American historical work, and no other book of its kind has had such ups and downs of fortune. Franklin lived for many years in England, where he was agent... *Biographies/History Pages 332*

Name	
Email	
Telephone	
Address	
City, State ZIP	

☐ Credit Card   ☐ Check / Money Order

Credit Card Number	
Expiration Date	
Signature	

Please Mail to: Book Jungle
PO Box 2226
Champaign, IL 61825
or Fax to: 630-214-0564

ORDERING INFORMATION
web: *www.bookjungle.com*
email: *sales@bookjungle.com*
fax: *630-214-0564*
mail: *Book Jungle PO Box 2226 Champaign, IL 61825*
or PayPal *to sales@bookjungle.com*

Please contact us for bulk discounts

DIRECT-ORDER TERMS

**20% Discount if You Order
Two or More Books**
Free Domestic Shipping!
Accepted: Master Card, Visa,
Discover, American Express

www.ingramcontent.com/pod-product-compliance
Lightning Source LLC
Chambersburg PA
CBHW081331040426
42453CB00013B/2373